Red Ants and Rainbows

Lily Kozee

BookLeaf
Publishing

Presentation by *BookLeaf Publishing*

Web: www.bookleafpub.com

E-mail: info@bookleafpub.com

ISBN: 9789395784474

First edition 2023

DEDICATION

This, my first published book, is dedicated to
Buddy, the best dog in the world.

ACKNOWLEDGEMENT

Thanks to my parents for reading all of my poems and telling me they were good. Thanks to Nana for the nature walks that inspired many of these poems. Thanks to my sister, Grace, who went on adventures with me & helped me see the world, both large and small. Thank you for reading my poems.

The Ant

I killed an ant today he
was resilient i'd say i'm
writing this at my desk
today I killed an ant as
he crawled away

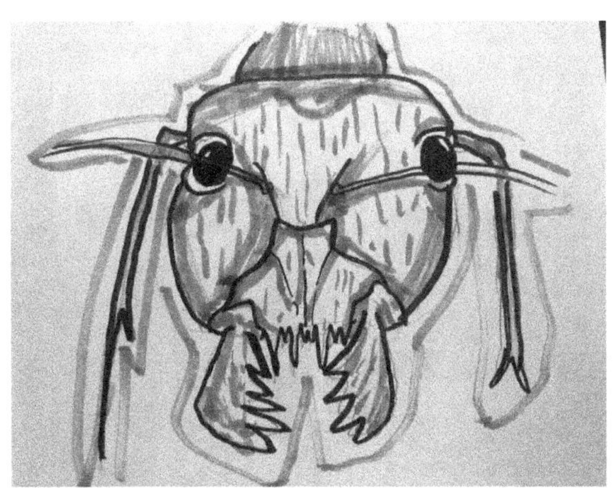

Scare Crow

I am a scarecrow
i don't walk i
don't talk. slim
and silent, thin
and idle i am
a scarecrow
none will see

Fade away

everyone fades
away sometime
a bird you sang
your song for
all to hear but
now it's passed
like a ring in
my ear we all
fade that's true
but what happens
after, a new song
to sing or nothing
to do

Girl

Watch out for the
girl is watching
you watch out for
the girls is stalking
you watch out
for the girl is
behind you
never mind she
already got rid
of you.

Dying

Passion fiery and red the
souls of whom are dead always
come to an end.

Come out, come out

behind this wall who are you
are you big and tall or
short and stout or are you
raging and roaring or are you
quiet as a mouse

Living

Green as grass and brass engraved
in your laugh green unlike the
sea lives like you and me

My Dog

your nose as
big as a button
and as black as
your eyes you
lift them up
toward the skies sun
shines down on
your sweet burnt
orange making you
as gold as your
goals you sniff
the flowers that
meet your eyes
big and brown
full of life you're
sweet and soft
and stinky too
but you're my
dog and i love
you and hope
you do too

Constellations

on this starry night
i look up to the starry
sky my eyes ever
so mesmerized
by this starry
night connecting
every constellation
right before my
eyes is this a
dream or did
i fall into
my fantasies.

Ghost Girl

ghost girl she watches
you sleep ghost girl
she watches you eat
ghost girl isn't a ghost
she's just a creep

Red

Red like roses
so sweet
red like a devil
from down beneath
red like blood
from a crime
scene red like
rubies oh how
they shine red
like fire when
it burns and
red is the color
that comes before
all of the others
it's the start
of the rainbow
so red is a ruler
a king a queen
red is a color
or so unique

Purple

Purple like a rare sunset
sky purple like lavender blooming
in spring purple like coral in the
deep blue sea purple like the English
 lady and lad's gown because
purple is the ruler of all
other colors with its lavender
scent and calming color along
with its great fashion make
a great ruler.

The Earth

The Earth is big we are
too we tower over many things
not the ocean blue the ocean's
big the Earth is too what is bigger the
Universe!

Cranberry Cascade

Frosty and furious the
Flame is lit frozen atop
its icy tip melting down
a smell so stiff.

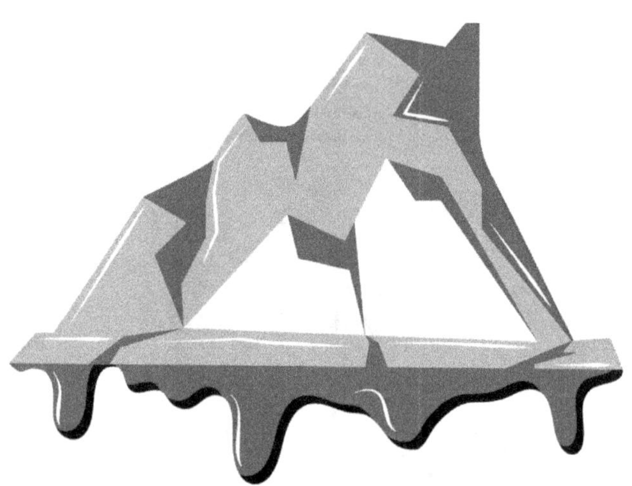

Religion

is money what makes
the world go round
or little men in the
clouds

Life

time trickles down
wood is carved time
is sound

Games

shocked and scared run
away shocked and happy
oh hurray!

21

21 days 21 ways to express myself
for pay